MW00423930

CHRISTIAN COMMUNITY

LifeChange

A NAVPRESS BIBLE STUDY SERIES

A life-changing encounter with God's Word

CHRISTIAN COMMUNITY

God's Word gives us vision and hope for what it means to be family in Christ.

NavPress

A NavPress resource published in alliance with Tyndale House Publishers

NavPress is the publishing ministry of The Navigators, an international Christian organization and leader in personal spiritual development. NavPress is committed to helping people grow spiritually and enjoy lives of meaning and hope through personal and group resources that are biblically rooted, culturally relevant, and highly practical.

For more information, visit NavPress.com.

Christian Community: A Bible Study on Being Part of God's Family

A NavPress resource published in alliance with Tyndale House Publishers

Written by Jack Kuhatschek

The Team:
David Zimmerman, Publisher; Caitlyn Carlson, Editor; Elizabeth Schroll, Copy Editor; Olivia Eldredge, Operations Manager; Sarah Susan Richardson, Designer

For information about special discounts for bulk purchases, please contact Tyndale House Publishers at csresponse@tyndale.com, or call 1-855-277-9400.

ISBN 978-1-64158-523-1

Printed in the United States of America

28 27 26 25 24 23 22
7 6 5 4 3 2 1

CONTENTS

HOW TO USE THIS STUDY

Objectives

The topical guides in the LifeChange series of Bible studies cover important topics from the Bible. Although the LifeChange guides vary with the topics they explore, they share some common goals:

1. to help readers grasp what key passages in the Bible say about the topic;
2. to provide readers with explanatory notes, word definitions, historical background, and cross-reference so that the only other reference they need is the Bible;
3. to teach readers how to let God's Word transform them into Christ's image;
4. to provide small groups with a tool that will enhance group discussion of each passage and topic; and
5. to write each session so that advance preparation for group members is strongly encouraged but not required.

Each lesson in this study is designed to take forty-five minutes to complete.

Overview and Details

The study begins with an overview of Christian community. The key to interpretation for each part of this study is content (what is the referenced passage *about*?), and the key to context is purpose (what is the author's *aim* for the passage as it relates to the overall topic?). Each lesson of the study explores an aspect of biblical community, with a corresponding passage from the Bible.

Kinds of Questions

Bible study provides different lenses and perspectives through which to engage the Scripture: observe (what does the passage *say*?), interpret (what does the passage *mean*?), and apply (how does this truth *affect* my life?). Some of the "how" and "why" questions will take some creative thinking, even prayer, to answer. Some are opinion questions without clear-cut right answers; these will lend themselves to discussions and side studies.

Don't let your study become an exercise in knowledge alone. Treat the passage as God's Word, and stay in dialogue with Him as you study. Pray, "Lord, what do You want me to see here?", "Father, why is this true?", and "Lord, how does this apply to my life?"

It is important that you write down your answers. The act of writing clarifies your thinking and helps you to remember what you're learning.

Study Aids

Throughout the guide, there are study aids that provide background information on the passage, insights from a commentary, or word studies. These aids are included in the guide to help you interpret the Bible without needing to use other, outside resources. Still, if you're interested in exploring further, the full resources are listed in the endnotes.

Scripture Versions

Unless otherwise indicated, the Bible quotations in this guide are from the New International Version of the Bible. Other versions cited are the English Standard Version, the New Living Translation, the Revised Standard Version, and the New Revised Standard Version.

Use any translation you like for study—or preferably more than one. Ideally you would have a good, modern translation such as the New International Version, the English Standard Version, the New Living Translation, or the Christian Standard Bible. A paraphrase such as *The Message* is not accurate enough for study, but it can be helpful for comparison or devotional reading.

Memorizing and Meditating

A psalmist wrote, "I have hidden your word in my heart that I might not sin against you" (Psalm 119:11). If you write down a verse or passage that challenges or encourages you and reflect on it often for a week or more, you will find it beginning to affect your motives and actions. We forget quickly what we read once; we remember what we ponder.

When you find a significant verse or passage, you might copy it onto a card to keep with you. Set aside five minutes each day just to think about what the passage might mean in your life. Recite it to yourself, exploring its meaning. Then, return to the passage as often as you can during the day for a brief review. You will soon find it coming to mind spontaneously.

For Group Study

A group of four to ten people allows the richest discussions, but you can adapt this guide for other-sized groups. It will suit a wide range of group types, such as home Bible studies, growth groups, youth groups, and workplace Bible studies. Both new and experienced Bible students, and new and mature Christians, will benefit from the guide. You can omit or leave for later any questions you find too easy or too hard.

The guide is intended to lead a group through one lesson per meeting. This guide is formatted so you will be able to discuss each of the questions at length. Be sure to make time at each discussion for members to ask about anything they didn't understand.

Each member should prepare for a meeting by writing answers for all of the background and discussion questions to be covered. Application will be very difficult, however, without private thought and prayer.

Two reasons for studying in a group are accountability and support. When each member commits in front of the rest to seek growth in an area of life, you can pray for one another, listen jointly for God's guidance, help one another resist temptation, assure each other that each person's growth matters to you, use the group to practice spiritual principles, and so on. Pray about one another's commitments and needs at most meetings. If you wish, you can spend the first few minutes of each meeting sharing any results from applications prompted by previous lessons and discuss new applications toward the end of the meeting. Follow your time of sharing with prayer for these and other needs.

If you write down what others have shared, you are more likely to remember to pray for them during the week, ask about what they shared at the next meeting, and notice answered prayers. You might want to get a notebook for prayer requests and discussion notes.

Taking notes during discussion will help you remember to follow up on ideas, stay on the subject, and have clarity on an issue. But don't let note-taking keep you from participating.

Some best practices for groups:

1. If possible, come to the group discussion prepared. The more each group member knows about the passage and the questions being asked, the better your discussion will be.

2. Realize that the group leader will not be teaching from the passage but instead will be facilitating your discussion. Therefore, it is important for each group member to participate so that everyone can contribute to what you learn as a group.

3. Try to stick to the passage covered in the session and the specific questions in the study guide.

4. Listen attentively to the other members of the group when they are sharing their thoughts about the passage. Also, realize that most of the questions are open-ended, allowing for more than one answer.

5. Be careful not to dominate the discussion—especially if you are the leader. Allow time for everyone to share their thoughts and ideas.

6. As mentioned previously, throughout the session are study aids that provide background information on the passage, insights from a commentary, or word studies. Reading these aloud during the meeting is optional and up to the discussion leader. However, each member can refer to these insights if they found them helpful in understanding the passage.

A Note on Topical Studies

LifeChange guides offer a robust and thoughtful engagement with God's Word. The book-centric guides focus on a step-by-step walk through that particular book of the Bible. The topical studies use Scripture to help you engage more deeply with God's Word and its implications for your life.

INTRODUCTION

Created for Community

CHRISTIAN AUTHOR and psychologist Dr. Larry Crabb once wrote this about the importance of community for our health and well-being:

> Community matters. That's about like saying oxygen matters. As our lungs require air, so our souls require what only community provides. We were designed by our Trinitarian God (who is himself a group of three persons in profound relationship with each other) to live in relationship. Without it, we die. It's that simple. Without a community where we know, explore, discover, and touch one another, we experience isolation and despair that drive us in wrong directions, that corrupt our efforts to live meaningfully and to love well.
>
> The future of the church depends on whether it develops true community.[1]

During the early days of the COVID-19 pandemic in 2020, millions of people worked from home rather than in an office. Church attendance dwindled, and many worship services were viewed from home rather than in person. The community group that my wife and I attend, which normally meets in homes for dinner, Bible study, and prayer, was held on an online video platform. It was better than nothing, but just barely.

The impact of the pandemic extended well beyond our physical bodies. As one article stated:

> The recent Covid-19 pandemic has had significant psychological and social effects on the population. Research has highlighted the impact on psychological well-being of the most exposed groups, including children, college students, and health workers, who are more likely to develop post-traumatic stress disorder, anxiety, depression, and other symptoms of distress. The social distance and the security measures

> have affected the relationship among people and their perception of empathy toward others.[2]

Social isolation has such a devastating impact because, as Larry Crabb observed, God created us for community. At its heart, the Christian life is about relationships—loving God, our neighbors, and our brothers and sisters in Christ.

In this LifeChange study guide, we'll learn what life is supposed to be like in God's family. Each session in the guide will focus on a key passage of Scripture that explores an aspect of Christian community and the context. There will also be suggestions at the end of each session for studying related passages.

As Christians, we are called to community relationships that are patterned after the eternal relationship between the Father, Son, and Holy Spirit. This LifeChange guide will help us catch the vision for what it means to live as the people of God.

Session One

THE NEW COMMANDMENT

1 John 3:11-24

THE WORD *love* can often feel overused. People love their favorite flavor of ice cream, their new tattoo, their college- or pro-football team, their spouse's new outfit, and even their brand of coffee. With such a watered-down view of love, is it any wonder that saying "I love you" may mean just the opposite: "I want you because you meet my needs"?

Instinctively, we all know that love—actual love—is something more that just mild affection or enjoyment. But often we are content to stay with the safe version, something that doesn't ask anything of us or require us to risk anything. Especially in community, which can be unpredictable and messy and painful, the risk of real love feels too great. But for people who follow Jesus, the reward of real love, lived out in Christian community, is worth the risk.

In this passage, John provides a clear contrast between what love is and what it isn't. He also describes how the supreme example of love equips us to enter community with hearts set together on the way of Jesus.

1. Read 1 John 3:11-24. John tells us that loving one another is a message we have heard "from the beginning" (verse 11). What do we learn about that message from Matthew 22:36-40 and John 13:34-35?

Jesus' "new command" (John 13:34-35) is not merely a restatement of "Love your neighbor as yourself." First, it has a new object: "Love one another," meaning other Christians in the family of God. Second, Jesus raises the standard from "as yourself" to "as I have loved you." His sacrificial death has become the model of the kind of sacrificial service that defines the meaning of Christlike love.

2. What does John tell us about Cain's actions, motive, and spiritual condition (see verse 12)?

Gary Burge tells us that "in Christian literature (Heb. 12:24; Pseudo-Clementine Homilies) the Cain and Abel story is generously used, particularly as a foreshadowing of the martyrdom of Christians. Abel's sacrifice was pleasing to God; Cain's was not. In the Christian church, the envy and revenge harbored by Cain were compared to the feelings of the opponents of Christians, whose sacrificial lives were pleasing to the Lord."[1]

3. How do we see attitudes and actions reflective of Cain and Abel in our society (see verses 13-15)?

4. Jesus is the supreme example of what it means to love each other (see verse 16). How did He do this throughout His life and through the cross?

5. How can we practically live out this model of love for our brothers and sisters in Christ (see verses 17-18)?

6. The NRSV links verse 18 with what follows: "Dear children, let's not merely say that we love each other; let us show the truth by our actions. Our actions will show that we belong to the truth, so we will be confident when we stand before God. Even if we feel guilty, God is greater than our feelings, and he knows everything" (1 John 3:18-20, NRSV). How does showing "the truth by our actions" reassure our hearts that we truly know God (see also verse 14)?

"John's words of assurance are linked to the foregoing exhortation about love. 'In this' (NIV, 'This then') should be taken as pointing backwards to verses 11-18, so that when the crisis of self-examination comes, the first evidence of our security with God is our obedience to the command to love. The NIV makes the verb tense present ('we know') when it is actually future. In other words, John is equipping his church, planning for a future episode when self-doubt and self-incrimination might paralyze them."[2]

7. When our hearts condemn us, John writes, we must realize that "God is greater than our hearts, and he knows everything" (verse 20). Why does the reality of God's greatness and omnipotence help our hearts rest?

8. How do both our actions and our hearts have an impact on our prayers (see verses 21-22)?

9. How does John summarize God's commands and the assurance that comes from following them (see verses 23-24)?

Gary Burge states: "The astonishing statement in verses 21-22 echoes other similar forms of confidence found in passages such as John 14:13-14; 16:23-24: *Whatever we ask will be given to us!* John says much the same in 1 John 5:14-15, but there modifies the statement with a condition: If we ask anything *according to God's will*, we will obtain what we ask. It is common in the Scriptures to find conditions attached to such promises: We must pray in Jesus' name (John 14:13) or abide/remain in Jesus and keep his commands (John 15:7). Here John says that we must do "what pleases him"; this presupposes a quality of intimacy that is in touch with God's very heart."[3]

10. Why is the kind of love John describes so crucial for the health of Christian community?

Your Response

In what practical ways can you meet the needs of your brothers and sisters in Christ on a regular basis?

For Further Study

Read 1 Corinthians 13. How does this chapter deepen your understanding of Christlike love?

Session Two

CARING FOR EACH OTHER

Philippians 2:1-11

HENRI NOUWEN WAS a popular and successful professor at Harvard Divinity School, following years of renown as a priest, lecturer, and writer. His role at Harvard was what many would consider the much deserved recognition of a life of significance: teaching only one semester a year to accommodate his travel schedule and fame. But as he paid attention to his heart and soul, he realized his lack. He longed for community. "After twenty-five years of priesthood," he wrote, "I found myself praying poorly, living somewhat isolated from other people. . . . I was living in a very dark place. . . . The term 'burnout' was a convenient psychological translation for a spiritual death."[1]

Most would have seen this burnout as an invitation to rest, to do some so-called self-care. But Nouwen did something different. He began to serve in the L'Arche community, living among and caring for people with disabilities. There "his life was transformed" through friendship with and service to those around him.[2] And that is how he spent the rest of his life.

Caring for others is an invitation to abundant life. When we lay down our privilege and self-focus and choose to serve those around us, we are following the example of our Savior, who showed us what it means to serve.

1. Read Philippians 2:1-11. What characteristics of Jesus are we called to share in this passage?

2. What do you observe about the role of the Trinity (Father, Son, and Holy Spirit) in this passage?

3. Why do you think Paul prefaces his exhortations to the Philippians with a series of "if" statements about their relationship with Christ and the Holy Spirit (see verse 1)?

4. Paul knows that the Philippians are experiencing "the same struggle" (1:30) that he is. How can "being like-minded, having the same love, being one in spirit and of one mind" (Philippians 2:2) enable them to endure those struggles?

5. How has the Christian community been able to help you during difficult times?

Frank Thielman writes: "The word 'if' does not mean that the Philippians' possession of the qualities that Paul lists is hypothetical. The Greek word for 'if' used here (*ei*) can sometimes mean 'since.' Because Paul does not doubt that the Philippians have experienced, for example, the 'encouragement' and 'comfort' of Christ, the word clearly has this meaning here. Paul's appeal, then, is based both on his friendship with them and on the blessings that belong to them because they belong to Christ."[3]

6. According to Paul, what are the contrasts between a self-centered and an others-centered mindset (see verses 3-4)?

Jac Müller states: "Nothing must be done or contemplated from selfishness or conceit. There must be no self-seeking, no sinful egotism; and also no conceit or pride....

"'Such a mind,' furthermore, is adverse to the spirit of unity in the church, for it seeks itself and breaks up the fellowship. Instead of this each should in humility count the other better than himself. Humility, a modest opinion of oneself, meekness, and an insight in one's own insignificance, is the opposite of self-exaltation, and it counts the other . . . better and more excellent than himself. Such a disposition will promote unity, for it binds believers together in mutual interest, respect and appreciation."[4]

7. Give examples of how you might value others above yourself and put the interests of others above your own interests (see verses 3-4).

8. Step by step, how did Jesus demonstrate that kind of humility in his incarnation and time on earth (see verses 5-8)?

9. What contrasts do you see between Christ's humiliation (see verses 6-8) and his subsequent exaltation (see verses 9-11)?

The second phrase in verse 6 has been translated a variety of ways: "did not count equality with God a thing to be grasped" (ESV, RSV), "thought it not robbery to be equal with God" (KJV), and "did not think of equality with God as something to cling to" (NLT). Frank Thielman writes: "This phrase is notoriously difficult because it represents a Greek word (*harpagmos*) that appears nowhere else in the Greek Bible and occurs only rarely in secular Greek. Its few secular occurrences carry the meaning 'robbery' or 'rape,' and so the KJV translated the phrase 'thought it not robbery to be equal with God.' Careful research has shown, however, that the word *harpagmos* could be used synonymously with the much more frequent word *harpagma*, and that both words appear in expressions similar to the one in Philippians 2:6 to mean 'an advantage.'"[5] Therefore, the NIV translates it as, "did not consider equality with God something to be used to his own advantage," and the CSB says, "did not consider equality with God as something to be exploited."

10. What Paul implies, Peter states explicitly: "Humble yourselves, therefore, under God's mighty hand, that he may lift you up in due time" (1 Peter 5:6). How does this promise encourage you to serve others in your Christian community?

Your Response

What steps can you take this week to focus less on your own interests and more on the interests and needs of others?

For Further Study

Read Philippians 2:17-30. How do Paul, Timothy, and Epaphroditus demonstrate the same mindset that Jesus did during his time on earth?

Session Three

YOUR ROLE IN THE FAMILY

1 Corinthians 12

RECENTLY, WHILE BUILDING some shutters for my sister, I accidently touched the table saw blade with my left thumb (ouch!). Fortunately, the cut was not deep, but my thumb was so sore that I couldn't use it. The next day, my wife asked me to hold one end of some gauze so that she could replace my bandage. Somehow, while cutting the gauze with very sharp scissors, she accidently cut into my *right* thumb, which also became unusable! For nearly two weeks, I had difficulty doing even simple tasks with my hands because I couldn't use my thumbs.

If we want to participate in the fullness of life, every part of our body has to be working as it should. This is how it is in the body of Christ. We are different people with different gifts, skills, personalities, and circumstances, and God wants to use all of us, working together, for the fullness of life in His kingdom. In 1 Corinthians 12, Paul explains why every member of the body of Christ is necessary and why even those who may seem unimportant are essential.

1. Read 1 Corinthians 12. What key words and phrases jump out at you?

2. What do you observe in this passage about the interdependence of the body?

3. What do you think Paul means when he says, "No one can say, 'Jesus is Lord,' except by the Holy Spirit" (verse 3)?

What is the Spirit's role in our participation in the community of faith?

4. How do verses 4-6 emphasize both the diversity and the unity in the body of Christ?

Craig Blomberg writes: "Paul notes that no one can sincerely declare Jesus to be *anathema* [cursed] who is a true believer (v. 3a). Conversely, only Christians—those indwelt by the Spirit—can acknowledge Jesus as Lord (v. 3b). Here is the fundamental early Christian confession of faith (cf. Rom. 10:9-10), flying both in the face of pagan affirmations of some other deity or emperor as god and master and in the face of Jewish insistence that Yahweh alone merited the title."[1]

5. Biblical scholars agree that the gifts listed in verses 8-11 are not exhaustive (see also Romans 12:3-8; Ephesians 4:7-13; 1 Peter 4:10-11). How might these spiritual gifts have been exercised "for the common good" (verse 7)?

"Any study of the spiritual gifts should include not only 1 Corinthians 12–14 but Romans 12:3-8 and Ephesians 4:7-13 as well. None of the various lists of gifts Paul gives in these chapters is identical, suggesting that none of them, individually or together, is intended to be comprehensive. . . . The range of functions covered by Paul's various lists of gifts makes it likely that any combination of talents, abilities, and endowments, however suddenly given or leisurely cultivated, may qualify as spiritual gifts, if a believer uses them for God's glory and his work in the world."[2]

6. When we use our spiritual gifts to serve each other, what happens (see verse 7)?

How does this shift your perspective of serving the body of Christ?

7. In what ways does the body of Christ, like the human body, struggle to participate fully in God's work if all parts are not working together (see verses 12-14)?

8. Verses 15-20 focus on those who feel that they have little to contribute to the Christian community. How does Paul encourage such people?

9. Verses 21-26 focus on Christians who feel superior to others and look down on those whose gifts seem less important than their own. How does Paul challenge that kind of prideful attitude?

10. Do you tend to identify more with the group in verses 15-20 or the one in verses 21-26?

"Where there is seemingly less value, power, or honor in the body, compensation occurs to preserve relative equality. In fact, the true value of a particular body part is often inversely proportional to its outward appearance. When Paul speaks of weaker body parts (v. 22) he may be thinking of fingers or toes, or the less protected organs such as one's eyes. The 'less honorable' parts (v. 23a) may refer to internal organs, usually covered by clothing, since the verb for 'treat' can also mean 'clothe.' The 'unpresentable' parts (v. 23b) most naturally refer to genitalia and the excretory tracts."[3]

Explain why. How do Paul's words either encourage or admonish you?

11. In verses 27-31, Paul is not ranking various gifts according to their importance; that would contradict everything he has said in this passage. What is his primary emphasis?

Craig Blomberg tells us that "to take 'first,' 'second,' and 'third' in verse 28 as a ranking in significance would clearly violate the whole point of Paul's discussion thus far. So it is best to see in this enumeration a chronological priority (cf. Eph. 2:20). To establish a local congregation requires a church-planter. Then the regular proclamation of God's Word must ensue. Next teachers must supplement evangelism with discipleship and the passing on of the cardinal truths of the faith. Only at this point does a viable Christian fellowship exist to enable all the other gifts to come into play. Tongues may be last on the list because the Corinthians were overestimating their value, but it cannot be demonstrated that Paul assigned them any inherent inferiority."[4]

12. How might our relationships in the community of faith change if we saw each person as crucial to how we participate in God's work?

Your Response

Some people have difficulty identifying their spiritual gifts. If that is true of you, there is a simple solution. In what ways can you best *serve* others in the Christian community?

For Further Study

Read the passages mentioned in question 5: Romans 12:3-8; Ephesians 4:7-13; and 1 Peter 4:10-11. How do these passages enhance your understanding of the diversity and proper use of spiritual gifts?

Session Four

LEARNING TO WASH FEET

John 13:1-17

WHEN MY EXTENDED family gathers for Thanksgiving or Christmas dinner, the food options are endless. Different family members have spent hours preparing good things to eat, and we enjoy the dishes and each other's company around the table. But then comes the awkward moment. The meal is over, the dining room table needs to be cleared, and the kitchen needs to be cleaned. Who will take care of the mess?

I confess that my normal response is to avoid eye contact so no one gets the impression that I'm one of the volunteers. But Scripture makes it clear: Part of being in God's family is serving our brothers and sisters, even (and especially) in those things that are humbling and difficult. In John 13:1-17, Jesus demonstrates that if we want to follow His example, we should be willing to do the menial tasks that no one wants to do. He also points to the necessity of His upcoming crucifixion to demonstrate what serving one another will ask of us.

1. Read John 13:1-17. What events and relationships set the stage for what happens in this passage?

2. Which part of this passage is most challenging to you?

D. A. Carson writes: "Jesus' special knowledge of his Father's will for him, articulated in v. 1, is now repeated, but with two significant additions: he knew not only that the time had come for him to leave this world, but that *he had come from God* and that *the Father had put all things under his power*. With such power and status at his disposal, we might have expected him to defeat the devil in an immediate and flashy confrontation, and to devastate Judas with an unstoppable blast of divine wrath. Instead, he washes his disciples' feet, including the feet of the betrayer."[1]

3. In Jesus' time, foot washing was a task performed by slaves. How does John's statement in verse 3 set up the irony of Jesus washing His disciples' feet (see verses 4-5)?

4. How does Jesus use Peter's protest to reveal the ultimate meaning of washing his feet (see verses 6-8)?

"We must picture the disciples reclining on thin mats around a low table. Each is leaning on his arm, usually the left; the feet radiate outward from the table. Jesus pushes himself up from his own mat. The details are revealing: Jesus *took off his outer clothing, and wrapped a towel round his waist*—thus adopting the dress of a menial slave, dress that was looked down upon in both Jewish and Gentile circles."[2]

5. Peter's over-the-top response (see verse 9) indicates that he doesn't yet grasp what Jesus is saying. What does Jesus mean when He says that all of His disciples (except the one "who was going to betray him") are "clean" because they "have had a bath" (verses 10-11)?

6. If all true followers of Jesus are already "clean" (verse 10), then why do we still need Jesus to wash our feet (see also 1 John 1:9)?

D. A. Carson tells us that "Jesus' point, granted the longer text, is that the common experience of natural life has its counterpoint in spiritual existence: the person who has taken a bath, and who is basically clean, may nevertheless need to have his feet washed after a short walk on dusty roads, even though another bath would be superfluous. In the same way, the disciples have received the cleansing salvation, prospectively, by faith: *you are clean*, Jesus comments, and then adds, *though not every one of you*."[3]

7. John tells us that "when [Jesus] had finished washing their feet, he put on his clothes and returned to his place" and then asked, "Do you understand what I have done for you?" (verse 12). If Jesus asked you that question, how would you answer?

8. Jesus served the disciples through washing their feet just before demonstrating the highest form of love and service through His sacrifice on the cross. We probably won't be called to that kind of sacrifice for our brothers and sisters in Christ, but in what ways can we follow Jesus' example (see verses 13-16)?

9. In what ways might you "be blessed" (verse 17) if you regularly devote yourself to "foot washing" in the community of faith?

10. How does our participation in Christian community change when we view serving as a core part of what it means to be like Jesus?

Your Response

Give specific examples of how you might humbly serve others . . .

- in your family,
- in your neighborhood, and
- in your church.

For Further Study

Read Mark 10:45 and Acts 20:35. What more do you learn about Jesus' example of service? What are some tangible ways in which you might follow His example?

Session Five

STOP JUDGING EACH OTHER

Romans 14

IF YOU DO a Google search for "Christians disagreeing," you'll get endless results. Opinion pieces about why Christians are disagreeing. Articles about how Christians *should* disagree. Posts lamenting how division permeates the Western church. Jesus said we would be known by our love—but these days, we seem to be known by our disagreement.

The Bible clearly lays outs the core pieces of our faith and what it means to follow Jesus. But what about gray areas where godly Christians disagree? When I was young, many conservative Christians thought it was a sin to dance, go to movies, play cards, and engage in a variety of other practices. And this kind of line-drawing isn't a neutral thing—judgment is toxic to healthy community. In Romans 14, Paul urges us not to judge our brother or sister whose list of what they consider "sins" is less—or more—restrictive than ours.

1. Read Romans 14. What initial reasons does Paul give to his readers about not quarreling over "disputable matters" (verse 1; see verses 1-4)?

Who are the weak and the strong in this passage? Douglas Moo writes: "Most commentators conclude that the core of the dispute has to do with observance of the Jewish law. The weak were those—mainly Jewish Christians—who could not bring themselves to abandon the requirements of the law they had observed all their lives. They could not, as Christians, simply ignore the food laws, Sabbath observance, and so on. The strong, by contrast, felt no need to observe these laws. Most of them were undoubtedly Gentile Christians, although a few, like Paul himself (see the 'we' in 15:1), were Jewish Christians."[1]

2. What guidelines does Paul give for deciding what we can and cannot do as Christians (see verses 5-9)?

3. Why might the Gentile Christians in Rome have judged or felt contempt for the Jewish believers who still followed the traditions they had grown up with?

4. Why should the knowledge of "God's judgment seat" (verse 10; that is, Judgment Day) keep us from judging other believers (see verses 10-12)?

5. What does Paul mean when he tells us "not to put any stumbling block or obstacle in the way of a brother or sister" (verse 13; see also verses 14-18)?

"If we are to understand the point of this section as a whole, we must recognize that the phrase 'whose faith is weak' (lit., 'one who is weak with respect to faith') has a special nuance in this context. 'Faith' refers not directly to one's belief generally but to one's convictions about what that faith allows him or her to do. The weak in faith are not necessarily lesser Christians than the strong. They are simply those who do not think their faith allows them to do certain things that the strong feel free to do."[2]

Douglas Moo tells us that "The vivid imagery of the 'stumbling block' (*proskomma*) comes from the Old Testament (see esp. Isa. 8:14, quoted in Rom. 9:32); the same is true of the word *skandalon* (NIV 'obstacle'). It refers literally to a trap, but was used widely in the LXX [a Greek translation of the Old Testament] to refer to the cause of one's spiritual downfall (see esp. Lev. 19:14); it has this same sense throughout the New Testament (e.g., Matt. 13:41; 18:7; Rom. 9:33; 11:9; 16:17; 1 Peter 2:8). Paul's point is clear: Those who pride themselves on being strong should display their spiritual maturity by doing everything they can to avoid bringing spiritual downfall to a brother or sister."[3]

6. Is Paul saying that we should not do *anything* that another believer feels is wrong? Why or why not?

7. In what specific ways does Paul urge us to care more for our brothers and sisters in Christ than we do about what we consider to be our rights (see verses 13-21)?

8. What role should our conscience play in deciding what gray areas we can and cannot practice (see verse 23)?

9. Why is it best for the Christian community if we keep whatever we believe about these gray areas between ourselves and God (see verse 22)?

Your Response

In what areas do you tend to judge other Christians for not being as "enlightened" as you are? How might you shift your perspective and better love those who disagree with you on "disputable matters" (verse 1)?

For Further Study

Read 1 Corinthians 8. How does this passage further clarify the attitude the Lord wants us to have about our weaker brothers and sisters?

Session Six

FAMILY RULES

Colossians 3:1-17

IN HIS BOOK *All I Really Need to Know I Learned in Kindergarten*, Robert Fulghum writes,

> These are the things I learned:
> Share everything.
> Play fair.
> Don't hit people.
> Put things back where you found them.
> Clean up your own mess.
> Don't take things that aren't yours.
> Say you're sorry when you hurt somebody.
> Wash your hands before you eat.
> Flush.[1]

In healthy communities, people share an understanding of what their responsibilities are and how to treat one another. In the community of faith, we are increasingly growing toward Christ's example in how we interact in relationship. Paul, in his letter to the Colossians, urges Christ followers to reject their old way of life and to conduct themselves in ways that are both pleasing to God and uplifting for the Christian community.

---

1. Read Colossians 3:1-17. What phrases describe our relationship and connection to Christ?

____

____

____

____

____

2. What are the practices of the old self?

What are the practices of the new self?

3. What does Paul mean when he tells the Colossians that they have "died" in Christ (verse 3), "been raised with Christ" (verse 1), are "hidden with Christ" (verse 3), and will eventually "appear with [Christ] in glory" (verse 4)?

4. Why should each of the sins Paul mentions in verses 5-7 be "put to death" by every true Christian?

David Garland describes the structure of verses 5-17: "Paul first enumerates the vices of the old morality, which need to be renounced (3:5-9a). He then lists virtues of the new morality, which need to be embraced (3:12-14). A statement about the new creation in 3:9b-11 provides a bridge from the vices to virtues—virtues made possible because God has created in Christ a new humanity 'being renewed in knowledge in the image of its Creator.' The new creation enables the new morality, which, in turn, leads to the new worship in 3:15-17. Thanksgiving, an emphasis throughout the letter (1:3, 12; 2:7; 3:15, 17; 4:2), climaxes this section."[2]

"In Hellenistic Jewish literature, all of the sins of the pagan world were epitomized by references to their sexual immorality and their idolatry (see Rom. 1:18-32), and the two were interconnected. Idolatry had as its chief purpose to get some material advantage from the gods, and idol worshipers tried to manipulate them to that end. The lust for worldly possessions quickly elbows God from the center of our lives as it captivates our total allegiance. We cannot serve both God and mammon, and those who serve mammon cannot serve God (Matt. 6:24). Our desires sit on the throne of our hearts rather than God."[3]

5. When we become Christians, we discard our old way of life as though it were filthy clothing. Why are the practices mentioned in verses 8-9 destructive within the Christian community?

6. If we "have taken off" (past tense) our "old self with its practices" (verse 9), then why do we still need to "put to death" and "rid" ourselves (present tense) of these practices (see verses 5, 8)?

7. When we become Christians, we also "put on the new self" like a fresh set of clothes (verse 10; see also verses 11-14). How do these new attitudes and practices build "perfect unity" (verse 14) in God's family?

8. How does Paul's claim that we "have put on the new self" (past tense) fit with his assertion that the new self is "being renewed [present tense] in knowledge in the image of its Creator" (verse 10)?

David Garland explains: "Since the new '*is being* renewed,' we are always needing more renewal (see Rom. 12:2)—Paul's use of the present participle suggests continuous improvement (see 2 Cor. 3:18; 4:16-17; Phil. 3:21). . . .This enduring process explains the use of the imperative. The believer 'has been made Christ's own' and 'set on course,' but all must run the race tirelessly for themselves. Theological indicatives are the basis of the ethical imperatives: 'You are, now be!'"[4]

What does this renewal look like in our everyday lives?

9. How should "the peace of Christ," "the message of Christ," and "the name of the Lord Jesus" affect our lives together as Christians (see verses 15-17)?

10. In light of the entire passage, how should our lives in community be different because we have died and been raised with Christ?

Your Response

In what ways have your moral and spiritual life been different since you became a Christian?

What areas still need the most transformation? How have those things affected your relationships with other believers?

For Further Study

Ephesians 4:17–5:20 is the parallel passage to the one in Colossians. What additional detail do you learn from this passage about your old life versus your new life in Christ?

Session Seven

SIN AND FORGIVENESS

Matthew 18:15-35

WHEN MY SON, Chris, was three years old, he plucked the heads off every tulip in our front flower bed, leaving nothing but naked stalks. When I found out what he had done, I raised my voice and asked, "Christopher James, did you pluck the heads off our tulips?" He shook his head in protest. "No, Daddy!" I tried again and said, "If you tell the truth, I promise I won't punish you." He looked at me sheepishly and replied, "Even if I did it?"

Sometimes being forgiven for something we've done wrong seems too good to be true. But forgiving others—especially when they have done something to hurt us—is far from easy. When someone sins against us, we have a decision to make. We can hold their offense against them and cut them off completely because we feel too hurt or don't want to enter the discomfort of addressing the issue, or we can choose to forgive. In this passage, Jesus points us to address the break in relationship in a way that prioritizes forgiveness, unity, and reconciliation within your faith community.

1. Read Matthew 18:15-35. What do you observe about God's approach to sin in this passage?

2. What is the process for addressing sin with a brother or sister in Christ?

3. Why is it crucial to first approach your brother or sister privately rather than discussing the matter publicly (see verse 15)?

4. Deuteronomy 19:15 states: "One witness is not enough to convict anyone accused of any crime or offense they may have committed. A matter must be established by the testimony of two or three witnesses." How does this passage alongside Matthew 18:16 underscore the seriousness of the sin and the vital importance of "witnesses"?

Michael Wilkins states: "Such an encounter must be undertaken with privacy so that if it is resolved, no undue attention will be given to the tragedy of sin committed by a member of the community. The ultimate objective of the encounter is not punishment but restoration—winning over a brother so that he can be restored to the faithful path of discipleship."[1]

5. If every step to address the sin and seek reconciliation fails, Jesus says to "treat them as you would a pagan or a tax collector" (verse 17; see also 1 Corinthians 5:1-5). What do you think He means by this?

"Confessing disciples who live with unconfessed sin indicate by their lives that they are not truly members of Jesus' spiritual family and are not to be allowed to enjoy its fellowship. They should be treated as unbelievers, with the same compassion and urgency needed to encourage them to repent; they are not to receive the same openness to the inner fellowship of the community that is reserved for fellow disciples."[2]

Michael Wilkins clarifies verses 18-20: "The periphrastic future tense indicates that what Peter and the disciples do in this present age has already been determined by God.

"The church is the instrument of God, who alone can grant forgiveness of sin or consign a person to judgment. The passive voice of 'will have been bound' and 'will have been loosed' and the phrase 'in heaven' are Semitic circumlocutions for describing God's actions. But the church does have the authority to 'bind and loose,' that is, to declare the terms under which God either forgives or retains sins (cf. John 20:22b-23). Jesus' statement assures the church that God in heaven confirms its judgment on a sinning brother."[3]

6. When such a serious step of discipline has been taken by the church, what does Jesus say and mean about heavenly support (see verses 18-20)?

7. Verses 21-35 shift from church discipline to the question of how many times we must forgive someone who has sinned against us. How might Jesus' response to Peter's question have been startling to Peter and the other disciples (see verses 21-22)?

8. Jesus follows this teaching with a parable that illuminates the importance of forgiveness. In the story He tells, what contrasts do you see between the king and the wicked servant (see verses 23-30)?

9. What similarities do you see between the king and our heavenly Father (see verses 23-30)?

"The teaching within Judaism (based on Amos 1:3; 2:6; Job 33:29, 30) is that three times was enough to show a forgiving spirit. Rabbinic Judaism recognized that repeat offenders may not really be repenting at all: 'If a man commits a transgression, the first, second and third time he is forgiven, the fourth time he is not' (*b. Yoma* 86b, 87a). The Mishnah is even less forgiving: 'If a man said, "I will sin and repent, and sin again and repent," he will be given no chance to repent . . . for transgressions that are between a man and his fellow the Day of Atonement effects atonement only if he has appeased his fellow' (*m. Yoma* 8.9)."[4]

Michael Wilkins explains: "The exact monetary value is difficult to determine, because the 'talent' was not a coin but a unit of monetary reckoning. A silver talent was about seventy-five pounds, valued at six thousand denarii. Since a denarius was the equivalent of a day's wage for a common laborer . . . and if we use the year 2001's minimum wage of $5.15 an hour in the United States, a common laborer could expect $41.20 a day. A talent, therefore, would be worth approximately $247,200 (cf. 25:15). Altogether, therefore, the man owes at least two and a half billion dollars."[5]

10. How does this parable illustrate why those who have been forgiven by God must forgive others who sin against them?

11. Why is forgiveness essential in the community of faith?

Your Response

Are there specific people in your life who hurt or sinned against you? Although your feelings about them may run deep, and restoration of the relationship may not be wise or possible, why is it important for you to forgive them?

For Further Study

Read Matthew 6:14; Mark 11:25; Luke 6:37; Colossians 3:13; and Ephesians 4:32. What do you learn from these passages about sin and forgiveness?

Session Eight

ONE NEW HUMANITY

Ephesians 2:11-22

IN 1963, the Reverend Dr. Martin Luther King Jr. said, "It is appalling that the most segregated hour of Christian America is 11 o'clock on Sunday morning." All these years later, that is still our reality. A majority of Americans attend a church where "a single racial or ethnic group comprises at least 80 percent of the congregation."[1]

Paul tells us in Ephesians 2:11-22 that hostility and division among people of different ethnicities, nations, and classes are totally contrary to what God desires. As His people, we are called to actively break down walls, to love, and to humbly learn from our brothers and sisters so we may increasingly reflect God's own diversity in unity. God is creating a new humanity in Jesus Christ.

---

1. Read Ephesians 2:11-22. What words and phrases are used to describe those who are in Christ?

2. What contrasting ideas do you observe throughout this passage?

3. Prior to the coming of Christ, Gentiles were "excluded from citizenship in Israel," thus experiencing both social and spiritual barriers between them and God (see verses 11-12). How would you explain each of the following:

"called 'uncircumcised' by those who call themselves 'the circumcision'" (verse 11) "separate from Christ" (verse 12)

"excluded from citizenship in Israel" (verse 12)

"foreigners to the covenants of the promise" (verse 12)

"without hope" (verse 12)

"without God in the world" (verse 12)

4. How has Jesus changed the status of the Gentiles who are now "in Christ" (verses 13-15)?

5. How did Jesus' death on the cross accomplish the following (see verses 15-18):

"create in himself one new humanity" (verse 15)

make peace between Jews and Gentiles (verse 15)

reconcile both groups to God through the cross (verse 16)

Klyne Snodgrass tells us that "it is no afterthought that Gentiles are now included in God's purposes. This theme may be secondary in the Old Testament, but it is there. God's covenant with Abraham had in view the blessing of the Gentiles (Gen. 12:2-3), the prophets anticipate the day when Gentiles will stream to worship God in Jerusalem (esp. Isa. 2:2-4; 56:6-7; Jer. 3:17), and the Psalms assume all the nations should worship God (Pss. 22:27; 86:9; 117:1; 148:11). In Paul's understanding of the gospel, what had been secondary—the inclusion of the Gentiles—has *now* become primary."[2]

"put to death their hostility" (verse 16)

give both groups "access to the Father" (verse 18)

"Notice that the new being . . . is a *corporate* idea. Jesus Christ in his death and resurrection identified with and represented humanity. People are incorporated into him, and when he is raised to new life, a new being comes into existence, one in which people are one with Christ and one with each other in him. Grace not only connects us to God and Christ, it connects us to each other."[3]

6. To what extent does your Christian community reflect the "one new humanity" that Jesus has created through the cross (verse 15)?

7. How do the expressions "fellow citizens with God's people" and "members of his household" explain the nature of the relationship we now enjoy with God's people—and with God Himself (verse 19)?

8. What are the various components of the "holy temple" (verse 21) that God is building?

And what is their significance (see verses 20-22)?

Klyne Snodgrass states: "The 'foundation of the apostles and prophets' is capable of several nuances. Theoretically it could mean the foundation the apostles and prophets laid, the foundation they have, or the foundation they make up. Given that Christ Jesus is the cornerstone, almost certainly the intent is to refer to the foundation the apostles and prophets make up. They are *part* of the foundation on which the church exists. This verse shows in personified terms the respect Paul and others had for the Christian tradition (cf. 1 Cor. 15:3-4; Col. 2:6-7). The teaching of the apostles and prophets is the basis on which the church rests. All Christians, as part of the building, are founded on the revelation and instruction conveyed by these people."[4]

9. God's presence among his people resided initially in the tabernacle (see Exodus 40:34-35) and later in the temple (see 2 Chronicles 7:1-2). How did these temporary dwellings foreshadow God's ultimate goal and desire?

10. Recalling Martin Luther King Jr.'s statement shared at the beginning of this session, why do you think there is still such a gap between the heavenly reality and our earthly experience of community?

Your Response

What can you do to foster greater unity within your Christian community?

For Further Study

Read Revelation 21:1-8. How does John's vision enlarge your view of what awaits us in the future?

NOTES

INTRODUCTION

1. Larry Crabb in Randy Frazee, *The Connecting Church: Beyond Small Groups to Authentic Community* (Grand Rapids, MI: Zondervan, 2001), foreword.
2. Valeria Saladino, Davide Algeri, and Vincenzo Auriemma, "The Psychological and Social Impact of Covid-19: New Perspectives of Well-Being," *Frontiers in Psychology*, October 2, 2020, https://doi.org/10.3389/fpsyg.2020.577684.

SESSION ONE—THE NEW COMMANDMENT

1. Gary M. Burge, *Letters of John: The NIV Application Commentary*, ed. Terry Muck (Grand Rapids, MI: Zondervan, 1996), 160.
2. Burge, *Letters of John*, 163.
3. Burge, *Letters of John*, 164–165.

SESSION TWO—CARING FOR EACH OTHER

1. Henri Nouwen, *In the Name of Jesus: Reflections on Christian Leadership* (New York: Crossroad, 1992), 10–11.
2. "Henri Nouwen," L'Arche USA, accessed February 17, 2022, https://archive.larcheusa.org/who-we-are/henri-nouwen/.
3. Frank Thielman, *Philippians: The NIV Application Commentary*, ed. Terry Muck (Grand Rapids, MI: Zondervan, 1995), 96.
4. Jac J. Müller, *The Epistles of Paul to the Philippians and to Philemon* (Grand Rapids, MI: Eerdmans, 1955), 75.
5. Thielman, *Philippians*, 116.

SESSION THREE—YOUR ROLE IN THE FAMILY

1. Craig Blomberg, *1 Corinthians: The NIV Application Commentary*, ed. Terry Muck (Grand Rapids: Zondervan, 1994), 243.
2. Blomberg, *1 Corinthians*, 248.

3. Blomberg, *1 Corinthians*, 246.
4. Blomberg, *1 Corinthians*, 247.

SESSION FOUR—LEARNING TO WASH FEET

1. D. A. Carson, *The Gospel According to John*, The Pillar New Testament Commentary (Grand Rapids, MI: Eerdmans, 1991), 462.
2. Carson, *Gospel According to John*, 463.
3. Carson, *Gospel According to John*, 466.

SESSION FIVE—STOP JUDGING EACH OTHER

1. Douglas J. Moo, *Romans: The NIV Application Commentary*, ed. Terry Muck (Grand Rapids, MI: Zondervan, 2000), 447.
2. Moo, *Romans*, 448.
3. Moo, *Romans*, 459.

SESSION SIX—FAMILY RULES

1. Robert Fulghum, *All I Really Need to Know I Learned in Kindergarten: Uncommon Thoughts on Common Things*, 25th anniv. ed. (New York: Ballantine, 2013), 2.
2. David E. Garland, *Colossians and Philemon: The NIV Application Commentary*, ed. Terry Muck (Grand Rapids, MI: Zondervan, 1998), Colossians 3:1-17.
3. Garland, *Colossians and Philemon*, Colossians 3:1-17, 204–5.
4. Garland, *Colossians and Philemon*, Colossians 3:1-17, 206.

SESSION SEVEN—SIN AND FORGIVENESS

1. Michael J. Wilkins, *Matthew: The NIV Application Commentary*, ed. Terry Muck (Grand Rapids, MI: Zondervan, 2004), 618.
2. Wilkins, *Matthew*, 619.
3. Wilkins, *Matthew*, 620.
4. Wilkins, *Matthew*, 622.
5. Wilkins, *Matthew*, 623.

SESSION EIGHT—ONE NEW HUMANITY

1. Zenitha Prince, "Eleven O'Clock on Sundays Is Still the Most Segregated Hour in America," *Louisiana Weekly*, June 15, 2016, http://www.louisianaweekly.com/eleven-oclock-on-sundays-is-still-the-most-segregated-hour-in-america/.
2. Klyne Snodgrass, *Ephesians: The NIV Application Commentary*, ed. Terry Muck (Grand Rapids, MI: Zondervan, 1996), 128.
3. Snodgrass, *Ephesians*, 134.
4. Snodgrass, *Ephesians*, 137.

LifeChange

A NAVPRESS BIBLE STUDY SERIES

LifeChange Bible studies train you in good Bible study practices even as you enjoy a robust and engaging Bible study experience. Learn the skill as you study the Word. There is a study for every book of the Bible and relevant topics.

SINGLE COPIES AND BULK DISCOUNTS AT NAVPRESS.COM

CP1212